The Dedalus Press

Carraroe in Saxony

Philip McDonagh

Carraroe in Saxony

Philip McDonagh

The Dedalus Press
24 The Heath ~ Cypress Downs ~ Dublin 6W
Ireland

© Philip McDonagh and The Dedalus Press, 2003

Cover: Reproduction of "Dresden on the Elbe" by Bernardo Bellotto 1720-80 courtesy of the National Gallery of Ireland

ISBN 1 904556 07 8 (paper)
ISBN 1 904556 08 6 (bound)

Dedalus Press books are represented and distributed —
in the U.S.A. and Canada by **Dufour Editions Ltd.**, P.O. Box 7, Chester Springs, Pennsylvania 19425 —
in the UK by **Central Books**, 99 Wallis Road, London E9 5LN

The Dedalus Press receives financial assistance from
An Chomhairle Ealaíon, The Arts Council, Ireland.

Printed in Dublin by The Johnswood Press

Contents

Part One — ROME

Intersection	9
A Certain Airport	11
The Journey of the Liberator	12
The Sparrow	14
Transeuropean Express	15
Winter Robin	17
Sidetracked	18

Part Two — GENEVA

Daniela	21
Halloween	23
Monsoon Weather	24
Imogene	25
Geneva, November 5th 1980	27
Between The Lines	28
In Fluntern Cemetery	30
Catullus	31
A Shrug Of Leaves	32

Part Three — COPENHAGEN

Copenhagen	39
Brussels	41
Sankta Sunniva	42
Transit Passenger	45

Ithaca	48
The Trails	50
Pictures From Paris	51
A Visit To Loker Hospice Cemetery	53
Concord	54
Leaving West Berlin	55

Part Four — CARRAROE IN SAXONY   59

Part Five — INDIA

Mobilisation	69
This My Heart's Wilderness	70
The Last Maharajah Of Cochin	71
Kalapani	73
Nobody Likes To Be Born	78
Bewley's of Grafton Street	79
Madurai Mission	82

Notes

ROME

Intersection

The Roman cobble-stones, bare-fisted knuckles,
rumble the wheels of Aiden's *Deux Chevaux*.
We flap slow wings within the arrow-flow
of cars along the Lungotevere.

Is it the seeing white smoke, the density
of people in the Square, has merged us all?
Just and unjust, the battered and the sleek,
we skim at speed until our common spree

trips at the Sistine Bridge by traffic lights.
A quantum like the sun on travertine
prisms our thoughts. As players in a scene
cut short, we make acquaintance. Over there's

Tomás O Fiaich, Archbishop of Armagh,
his driver's window down, saluting us.
And now the slowly abdicating sun
picks out the dome of the basilica.

We wave in turn, installed, not cardinals,
but partisans in wonder. The affray
of cars moves on. It seems we know the way
and pick out berries on the hedge of time,

confecting them in sweet complicity;
and all that Father Tiber has observed
of sins and secrets since the She-Wolf bawled
on the Capitoline, a mighty sea

has purged. If John Paul Two, with hand-me-down
tackle from Galilean days, should throw
his dragnet from the Ponte Milvio
and grill a fresh haul for the cardinals

under Bernini's colonnade, our hope,
pristine as bread, would not be out-hoped. Time
that skives a sparrow in the palm, we say:
It isn't every day they make a Pope.

A Certain Airport

We had our dates and places
And a history too
But if that history mattered
I would still need you

Or else there lies a mystery
Behind love's rule
That reasons aren't requested
At her school.

But as I cannot understand
Should I forget, then,
The way you looked and where we went
The times we met?

The Journey of the Liberator

It was a long way to Genoa —

wet flagstones and the smell of fish
hard-handed girls
in taverns dark enough to shade faces
cloth on sale under the arches
and where larger deals have been transacted
the palaces of Spínola, Doria, Tursi.

The innkeeper said later,
"I had an old man dying here last week.
A gentleman. Couldn't eat his meals.
English, I think.
Complained about the noise below."

Far are the cliffs of Clare
the bar at Westminster
hallways in Dublin
cool with polished banisters
Assizes in Cavan
and people nodding in the sunlight afterwards,
"Eleven out of twelve men Dan saved from the gallows."

The Repeal, I have it in a box...

And there were homecomings to Derrynane,
how right to marry!

*and friends. Where were they
in all that clutter of life?*

The Repeal...

*Ireland, is it a country at all
and what is it I said that they loved me for it?
O God, you're calling out my name
the name of every ragged person that was or will be*

May God help them all.

No light from the shutters to vary the dry floorboards
a woman's voice in the street: Gianna! Gianna!
a cart's wheel
the day retiring without a word to the Ligurian hills.

At 16, via al Ponte Reale
a priest kneels
by the white-haired, vein-handed, still-hearted
Daniel O'Connell.

The Sparrow
(a version from Catullus)

You gods of love, you lovely things
Of man, lament the end
Of a simple creature; sparrow
Who was my darling's friend.
She loved him more than her own eyes,
For he was a delight,
And he knew her like a mother's son,
As well indeed he might,
For she would keep and cosset him
In her bosom, all day long,
Or hither and thither he'd hop about her,
Piping his little song.
He's on his way now, down the pitch
-black way beyond the tomb,
From where no traveller returns.
O Blinded, Wicked Gloom,
May it go ill with you for greed,
Whose meal is never through
Of gentle things; and snatched her sparrow
Who was gentle too.
A foul deed on a poor wee bird!
The sin is on your head
That in a flash a flood of tears
Has made her soft eyes red.

Transeuropean Express

Mother-to-daughter: you're three and a half
So you *ought* to be better and more polite
Than Giampaolo who is only one
— *Più brava e più gentile.*

Giampaolo, in dungarees, smiles at a fellow passenger
Closes his fist on the rim of a paper cup.
Water splashes the floor, splashes the biscuit crumbs,
And as the owner of the cup speaks quietly
A mother's hand swoops
Restraining the Pope's namesake
By a minimal use of force
And the silence is measured over again
By the pulsation of the wheels
Shove and we have it
Shove and we have it
Like the rugby cheer.

Morning light expands
In a valley of oyster-coloured rocks
A skyline the shell
Of a decapitated breakfast boiled egg.
The shoulders of her white cardigan
Droop from a peg.

At Brig the orange-coated railwaymen
Bustle convincingly

Their shapes a score of station-music
Noted on lines of track.

Mountains exhibit their point-work in the sun
And tracks pivot like a camera
To frame a hidden valley
A village like an illuminated page.
Then vines on stakes, fields combed,
Uneven walls of brick like ancient forts

Lake Geneva by morning
The transformation of the elements
One to the other
Water, air, earth, sun.

We skirt the water's edge
Alps to the South linen-draped with snow
The Northern Jura graciously standing back
To usher us in silent deft motion
Into the city of asylum
Geneva
Home — luxuriously appointed — of free thought.

Winter Robin
(after a Danish air)

All the world is snowing
Softly padding, whitely blowing
Everywhere is crisp and clean.
Winter robin, can you fly now,
Winter robin, must you die now,
Scratching at the frosty pane?

All the wood is bare
Swallow flown and fox in lair
Snow has buried autumn's leaves.
In the ceiling of the sky
Can you hear the raven cry
Can you tell for what he grieves?

Now the eagle's ranging
Do you feel the wind a-changing
Do you see the speckled fawn?
There are blossoms on your tree now
Winter robin, will you be now
Herald of tomorrow's dawn?

Sidetracked
(after the Spanish of Baltasar del Alcázar, 1530-1606)

To shameful passion, love-in-threes,
a prisoner I am
— to Isabel, and to smoked ham,
to aubergines in cheese.

I had no other gallantries,
Isabel's Tristram,
until she served me with smoked ham
and aubergines in cheese.

O vilest of polygamies!
But don't *chercher la femme*:
the sin lies mainly with the ham
and aubergines in cheese.

GENEVA

Daniela

Daniela is dark-haired, Italian
and she told Nick last year
she was twenty-nine, our age.
I called her once or twice,
and the second time, in the sitting area
of her large one-bedroomed apartment,
as we chatted over cheese, she drew the cork
from yesterday's Chianti
and said almost in passing
that she was planning a holiday.

A half-a-dozen conversations on
I still don't know
exactly what she does:
research of some kind, here in Geneva,
on a grant that soon runs out.
Last time, "Where have you been?" she said,
I kissed both cheeks,
and she and I and that boyfriend of hers
whose wife is in Brazil
laughed at Swiss particularness
and the difficulty she might face
renewing her *permis de séjour*.

We'll get together soon, the usual friends,
at Les Armures or La Glycine,
one of those places. Late on,

as words fall fast
and our stemless glasses
huddle like foothills
by the peak of a last bottle
of Aigle or Fendant
I won't recall, I'm sure,
that backstage world,
the blanket evenly spread
behind the bookcase on a low bed.

Halloween

The conversation is a Catherine wheel
fizzing, the wine flows fortified and free,
and I, corked black, daubed red, Mr. Surreal
himself, am scuba-diving in a sea

of cleavages — until remembrance mars
my thought, as at a roadstead freshening wind
depicts the arctic in a gauze of stars
and calls to mind a voyage. How rescind,

though, words that have been said? Her love I trust,
that was, and from this memory infer
tomorrow's acts of kindness: simple dust
that poor and scant and all, will bury her.

Monsoon Weather

The air was staggering in Manila's heat
As close to four P.M.
We crossed the roadway to the new hotel.
The rooms in which we meet

Are named for places in the Philippines
And here in the Salle Sulu
— "Salle" the Presidency being French —
The Community convenes.

"Thank you, Chairman. Looking at para. 4. . ."
Interpreters set to,
Mouth silent messages behind their glass,
The air-conditioning's roar

A cataract. As France's microphone
Sparks with a click to life, the member
States — "Danemark", "Allemagne", "Irlande" —
Are called on to intone

A chain of thought. A corridor away
In the blue-pooled bar-served garden
Residents and their guests, as servants watch,
Assuage the livelong day,

The stick that jogs the ice-cubes in the glass
Laid back
As the ocean idling behind its wall
Or towel upon the grass.

Imogene

Though I was twenty three
at most, eighteen seemed young;
and though I turned her way
to see that red hair slung
to the shoulder, yet her door
was distant, overhung

with hazard. Imogene,
simply to be a friend,
to take tea, walk with you
down by the towpath, blend
long hours and lazy words,
promised no dividend

to one who would lay out
in some bonanza all
his ill-earned passion. Once,
on New Year's Eve, your call,
your steady, "Good night, Philip,"
gave me the wherewithal

to dream. But in the town
I saw you walking late
on Erik's arm, and thought,
As well to extricate
myself in good time. Now,
my dreams without a mate

seven years on, I fear
the fool I may have been;
I fear fear, which walls up
a wildering demesne;
I hear Dad say again,
Why not phone Imogene?

Geneva, November 5th 1980

Between two and eight
the lady commentator
has changed her dress
but the note on which I went to bed
— that Reagan's in —
is inescapable
even in French.

At my Geneva widow,
coffee cup in hand,
I hear Carter's farewell.
A word to praise the system:
his bright bitter self-aware propriety
no match for Calvin's Cathedral,
pencil-drawn in early morning shadows.

Reagan, a professor says,
*has promised to return America
to the Americans. By which is hardly meant,*
he adds, *the Sioux Indians.*
Snow falls, the season's first.
It veils the giant catafalque
of the Intercontinental Hotel.

Between The Lines

In the name of justice
as though some rule were broken
I make a veiled complaint
not veiled
not really a complaint
but if you like a plea
that she spare me pain
and show me love
by not seeing this other friend
the one she's kissing still

and she, conscious that my words
carry no ultimatum,
speaks of the heart
— that most feminine quarter —
its tours in time
its universe
of living landscapes
and unpublished destinations,
and adds,
"But I would never use you."

So it's a truce now
under a rigged-up flag:
unscripted conscripts,
blithe
beneath emplacements,

knowing that the peace
can but be made, if peace come,
elsewhere and apart,
we learn to fraternise
between our lines.

In Fluntern Cemetery

Geboren Dublin; Zürich gestorben. So
Narrates a simple gravestone. Some blackbirds,
A squirrel sudden on the frozen snow,
An emptiness that greets you in those words.

Onwards the blue tram climbed that took me there
And higher; to one who had his eyrie dreamed
Above the Zürichsee, and breathed this air,
How poor and quarrel-stricken Dublin seemed.

And yet you shopped those streets, and Terenure
Is where the world was on your Christening Day,
James Joyce. Did something of that day endure
That when through some Swiss gate death pushed its way

It found a man of faith? A churchyard's loam:
To this poor Ithaca your heart came home.

Catullus

The most part earth not gold,
upended from heart's pit
— but un-foretold,

among abandoned seams
and empty passages,
an image gleams

rare as a cut flower, slain
red-coated officer
of the ranks of grain.

A Shrug Of Leaves

Encounter

I find you coming back to mind:
fresh fields remembering
a cloud that rained

or trembling clod of matter, spun
of a sudden into orbit
by some new sun.

Terms Of Credit

"Sunburn, sandals, see-through shirt
and hyacinthine hair:
well of mercy, fire of hurt —
darling, who goes there?"

"I promise this, if you attend
my heart's unsteady flame,
and only this, that come the end,
you'll utter soft my name."

Rose-window

Your silence
— a sail stubborn in the wind
in Barleycove bay
or what a rider knows,
his hand along the rein.

You come near
— light sudden and acceptable
as when I saw the sun
fulfil the rose-window
at Modena

or lay his accolade
at early morning
on Roman streets that knelt,
waiting.

    Rehearsal

Presentiment of kisses not yet known
is a ferment within
from which a clumsy verse
line by slow line is pressed.

A verse, though it keep a sweetness of its own,
covers the skin
of living. Why rehearse,
where heart and heart undressed?

    How long?

A slipper danced along the sand and shone
to marvel at, its legacy a wan
imprint above the tide; and at your gate,
in livery that turns to rags, I wait.

The Dialogue

A dialogue in Dante:
you, the pilgrim,
she, the soul
(in paradise, why not?),
and much as you may share
— searchlights of different colours
blending in the night
each source remote from the other —
you must move on
untouched
unhealed.

A Shrug Of Leaves

Dinner *à deux* is down to a debris
of crumbs. A not yet blossoming rose,
like General Custer's horse that galloped free
out of the massacre, would interpose
its own unscathedness; it turns on me
a sappy shrug of leaves. How well it knows
my contretemps, this rose her natural friend
— I mean the Unflushed One, who upped and went,
honing her words! Sharp rose, you comprehend
that to capsize before an argument
is to abandon beauty! Hours I spend
in dedicated hope, you represent!

The Tribute-payer

Pericles, at the Potters' Graveyard,
weighing the splendour of the City
against her soldiers' sacrifice,
proclaimed: "Alone of cities,
she ever will outdo expectation.
To be ruled by her — alone of cities —
is free of reproach, of the racking
bitterness of those who are subject."

You count as Athens then, count me
an ally, some tribute-paying island
at two days' sail, helpless before the blind
torrent of your politics, subdued
to think what skill, how many drachmae,
created the Acropolis:
I murmur, "Yes, but you are worthy,
but Athens is worthy to rule."

New World

She's gone as the glacier goes
that carries all away,
and severing, slips a new world
into the void of day.

Auspices

From her flights and her approaches
you took the auspices and got no sign
— which nullifies the scope

for imagining, for claiming
her friendliness gave you encouragement
or that an honoured hope,

disappointed once, might flourish
in season. Pleaded with, she'll not relent,
— you know this — but repeat

as though put upon, what softly
she said once. Dreams adulterate the wine
of truth: take failure neat.

COPENHAGEN

Copenhagen

At Hørsholm, Holte, and along the coast
the subfusc autumn colours of the trees;
by every bus-stop workers at their post
before the dawn, in silent companies;

the unforced elegance of market squares
and royal roofs flushed greener by the rain
as mid-day shoppers scuttle to the lairs
of gleaming galleries chock with porcelain;

and Langelinie, where that northern belle
poised on her rock forever for the gaze
of passers-by, waits; us she cannot tell
of her lost love; no glance, no smile betrays

half-memories of the night which saw her trace
her careful kisses on a storm-drenched face.

In Domus Vista high above the town
we crumble pastry to the undertow
of still remembered songs; and looking down
on Fredericksberg — within, the quiet glow

of special candles, snow-lanterns; outside,
lamp-light brocaded on the dark duvet
of night — we will forget the loveless tide
where mermaids dwell, and one, poor fiancée

of nothing but her pain, whom passion's touch
turned — little mermaid, though your brave display
merits a pedestal, self-giving such
as yours, so prompt, distresses us; today,

a girl's her own; if lovely, knows her due;
to all that is expected of her, true.

Brussels

Nostalgia: the pain of going back,
as I go back
led even by the camber of the streets
to find, among the spot-lit gilt façades,
that alcoved room
where we caught on together,
nothing again the same.

Upstairs and down I scan each table
(all are full)
wondering if you too hover at the scene,
a gentle ghost; but see only the others,
other eyes that meet
above hot wine and ginger biscuits,
re-making an old theme.

Sankta Sunniva

Watchful where we watch merely
they hug the channel's edge
their light craft plucked by that last cape
from the unsteady cauldron of the sea.
A woman bales patiently.
In water smooth beneath a pox of rain
she trails a finger.
Unless the sun comes through
there'll be no fire tonight.

On deck in our fast ferry
— trailing a coxcomb of spray
as we boom along the fjord —
the faces glow.
Evening is apportioned quietly
to ourselves
until the mountains near and far
are lost in the unlit rain
like nuances.

For you, Sunniva, lady of Selje,
the mountains were folds
never to be lifted
the headland a drape hung heavily
never to be drawn
on Ireland
on the gardens of the past.

A thousand years ago, an August night
the last of the sun
slipping like a veil
from a reach of westward-facing water
Sunniva among friends
murmurs of home, remembers faces.
Was it the God of Patrick
the Trinity
the God of monasteries
brought you here?
You think, "I could have had a husband"
but awake each dawn on Selje
to a pale sun
as a seed struggles to rise
in the hard acre in which it fell.

On the wet boreen
we tourists muddy our shoes,
a study for the black-nosed sheep
which inattentively share with four families
a domain of pine, heather, rock.
A dismal cave,
the platform of the first church,
the monastery tower
tell, tell of a torch once bright,
doused now by the rain of centuries.

Once the word flew among the towns of staves,
Håkon Jarl is dead: Olav is king.

In Kvæfjord, Bygland, Austevoll they said,
The men of Selje, of the new faith, who died,
are to be honoured,
Sunniva buried in the bishop's church,
friars in black come from Ireland, from England,
Westland has a saint, Norway its own saint.

Your life then long since hidden
all but a name
in its cave-tomb
under a curtain of stones.

Transit Passenger

    I
The shop takes dollars,
plastic, smiles.
Screens and consoles
are acquainted with your case.
Everything is confirmed.
Boards click above your head
— Osaka Mumbai Riyadh Perth.
In the whale's belly
of the business class lounge,
you hide behind
the Asian Wall Street Journal,
drinks complimentary,
the music built in.

    II
Mind slips downmarket.
At Klampenborg racecourse,
the April sunlight salted with rain,
we children in yellow anoraks
study horses' feet
in the black clay of the parade ring.
In a major city of culture
Simon gains admission to the opera
on presentation of a docket
from the automated parking lot.
The snow falls in Grande Place.
Moyra faces me,
her hair dark as a cello.

We're in the Roi d'Espagne,
more between us than mulled wine.

    III
Memories are neither bonds nor ingots,
and from their promissory pain
we derive nothing
— thus, in all civility,
as flights are called,
the Singaporean air conditioning
reminds us.
On the Sarawak's brown waters,
gondolas under the rain,
their transit skewed.
Ferrymen:
Matchsticks, blackened,
jettisoned at random.
The caucusing
of a hundred hundred birds.

    IV
Two men are travelling together,
a young man, Indian,
and a companion, wheelchair-bound,
the red rims of blindness
buckling his eyes.
The companion is from Ireland.
"Going home?" I ask.
"My home is India. Since 1933.
Before that, Athenry."

"You mean. . .?"
"I'm in the Brothers."
"So for three-quarters of a century. . ."
"In the Gangetic valley, yes.
Maybe something" — the old man floats away —
"maybe something's written in the book."

    V
Later a river spumes
rushing by *ghats* at sundown
bearing boats of light.
I begin my journey,
rain pummeling the waters,
pulling punches.
Land's edge recedes.
The boatman,
barefoot among boxes,
non-descript as nightfall,
desires of me:
Trade in the softest of currencies,
the non-transferable roubles
of the heart.

Ithaca
> (*after Giovanni Jannuzzi in his collection* Ritorno ad Itaca, *Firenze Libri, 1987*)

Musical is their night-sound, song
of the sirens, summons to a shore
of ease: "Ulysses,
who have tested and been tested,
nothing so full, know this,
exists as here."
The wind billowing the sheets fails,
Ithaca a point
within the uncoordinated space
of man's heart.

A lavish landfall:
and out of caves
the lapping and overlapping voices come,
"Be content, Ulysses,
with what is granted here.
A never-charted sea surrounds
your island. To those who journey on,
her look turns bitter-strange.
Future has no being, past
has introduced you to our presence,"
— so sing these voices —
"you yourself the obstacle
to all that is to be encompassed
once you bide here,
abandoning the sea."

Fearing this fear-dissolving melody
the wanderer
expert of many battles
has his men grapple him to the mast.
His bonds grip.
There in the darkness
he gives the word:
Strike the sea-roads.
It's hard,
holding a rudder to the stars,
troubling the cold wave with busy oars.
But Ulysses will sail on.
Ithaca is a lamp lit
within the inner room of a temple
and is not extinguished.

The Trails

Remember the blue pistes in spring?
The winds touched us as we schussed,
then sudden somersaults
and back to the top
under beaming Alps.

On the red we could manage
using side-slips and stem-turns,
muscles coming out of atrophy
as we tugged at gravity
on steepy embossed hillsides.

Now I've strayed onto black.
With snow falling I see no one.
There's no technique.
The crevasse a serpent's jaw.
A helicopter impossible.

Pictures from Paris

I close my eyes,
voyager come to a far cave
where heat hovers
under the dry leaves of the tamarind:
tugging at the anchor of a name.

A footfall rumoured in the room beyond.
The reticence of a purple lamp
does not conceal a nightdress, discarded,
radioactive with scent.

At evening, in a parked car,
"Ça recommence," you mutter.
I raise my voice
you interrupt
we contradict ourselves
in an unlikely quarter of the city.
"You are a stranger," I hear,
and, "I have no more chances to give,"
and, "It is a kind of surgery."

You would not be kissed in the morning
and I picture you
composed in a cotton robe;
on the table on your balcony
a bowl of tea, some letters,
Madame Figaro.

A dispassionate sun
parches the wells of shade.
Marooned among shadows
in St - Germain - des - Prés,
I grope heart-wise
towards deliverance.

A Visit To Loker Hospice Cemetery, 1990

"Well done, lads," writes Fitzpatrick, ninety-four,
veteran, in script like barbed wire all these years
on, rain cavorting down as we ignore
the one the other. Thus at Armenteers,
Pop, Wipers, Shelltrap Farm, one could dispense
with names and packdrill for a soldier's far
intimacy, the enabling reticence
of those about to die, whose graves these are.

Redmond, I find, is buried separately.
The lives lost here would help us to agree,
he dreamt, in Ireland, North with South, and win
Englishmen's trust. The Ulsters brought him in,
grey-haired, soon after dawn. In this mute space,
his one man's no-man's land, he rests his case.

Concord
*(a version of the poem by Giovanni Jannuzzi in his
collection* Stazione di Frontiera, *Firenze Libri 1989)*

On tip-toe, wheels to the ground,
it shudders
— beasts of prey are poised like this —
then races the runway's length, rears up,
is loosed into the air, crossing
the lead-shaded heaviness of cloud
to bolt into clear blue,
weightless, without sound. Above,
in geostationary orbit, satellites
having the ancient names of gods
keep watch, cold unmoved divinities
that are the children of men.
The new world beginning
feeds on vastness, disdains
our worn everyday littleness,
skips frontiers, calls mankind
to new covenants, in a common home.

Leaving West Berlin

The trains departing East
are notified in chalk
as though to cross the line
to Friedrichstrasse

is never planned or certain.
You say, "Let's walk,"
but where the August light
begins, we stand,

you uttering the words
that rise later
within me, a steadfast moon
distantly bright.

Approaching Prague, the train
swings before dark
into a valley, the carriages
an arc

like the sweep of an hidalgo's cape
long-folded,
liberating from a place of dust
a golden weave;

and it seems my heart comes to
amid the scent

of a multiform regiment
of flowers, not one

but hints 'Jill'; and I hear
the whispered words
I could give back to you,
my travelling done.

But now the track once more
straightens, seals
the cape the sun flattered
within a store

where cloth fades; the wheels
involve my senses;
and by the local light at my shoulder
I check my documents.

CARRAROE IN SAXONY

In summer 1988
the restaurant, commended by
a friend as fit for honeymoons
and westerners, is Dresden's best.
The Wall impends, accounting for
the too-Germanic menu, why
the roads are quiet, the charisma
a foreigner has entering
this place. Day dims, as if a slow
wheel modulates the light, until
the vase-like spires turn monochrome.
I read a book on barricades,
the workers' cause. When I look up,
the lanterns of the Elbterrasse
are multiplied on glass. They glow,
like meanings in a sacred text
returned to after silence. There,
dishes that sizzle on their pans
have been prepared, the menu says,
"in a Lucullan way." *Defend
the moments of no consequence*,
you used to say; and such is this.

You would have wished me not a few
but myriad illuminations
— you, Ma, for whom the grave was dug
nine weeks ago tomorrow. Dresden
for you was distant, an extreme
wonder. But you had a mind
to see the Giant's Causeway, and
along the Antrim coast Portrush,
where Uncle Vincent drowned. You saw

the whole of it in any case
walking the quiet road that made
a shortcut from the *Caorán Mór*
to *siopa Nancy* and then, the gorse
behind you, down to the heart's own
metropolis of Carraroe.

As haystack-yellow as her hair
the Rhine wine that a waitress pours
without stint — *Thank you* — *Bitte schön* —
as memories return: of you
humping the shopping bags the length
of Greenmount Road, as full as you
could make them of the makings of
hamburger buns; then you and Dad
on duty half the night, a Krupps
down in the kitchen, turning out
matériel: chips, onions, burgers,
that gilded youth, crammed willy-nilly
into the living room upstairs,
accepted like a compliment.
The end was coming and you crossed
New York, the winter closing in,
angina doubling the cost
of everything, to hear Charles Curran,
dissenting theologian. But
you'd skip Mass, talking about saints
and how they mortify the flesh
and how for us the thing to do
is, *mortify our consciences.*

This week in Dresden, to permit
my grief, I sought the shade of churches.
In one, a cyclorama plain
as daylight forms a backdrop to
activity. A hammer-tap.
A clunk on stone as a hauled rope
loaded for leverage is let slip.
Sporadically someone on
the organ practising. Three men
portering great tureens of whitewash
along the aisle, me following
duly, the tiles grey-white, grey-white,
as in a game of chess — to find,
within a chapel's vaulted space,
a marble altar where the prayer
rebuffed one February night
in 1945 is written
high on the wall. Those workmen's world
— to paint, fix, bustle, take the tram
on Sunday to the river down
still streets — checkmated, as I try
deciphering a plaque on which
a date in 1932
is mentioned. Suddenly a well
is driven in my heart but out
springs nothing — save, in mind's ear, noise.
Deep-throated aircraft loping in,
Dresden a place-name on their charts,
as captains, flat-eyed pantomimes,
commune on crackling radios.
Hysteria in heaven's womb.
Efflux of metal. Draught of fire.

Then every mother's child consumed,
gashed, bloodied, by the claws of heat.
Old Dresden smashed like porcelain.

The music in the Elbterrasse,
from *Cats*, becomes an elixir.
A man rides high, reality
an amphitheatre, the stones
we sit on booty out of some
Jerusalem, and only fools
will eke their lives out slavishly,
not penetrate to where the rules
are made. I notice her: the Wine
— maiden in split black skirt, heels raised
as on a starting-block. She smiles,
the havering confusion gone,
a butterfly alighting softly,
pert among petals. Twenty-two
or three seems old enough. I pause,
request more wine. A part of me
entreats, "But give an Irish girl
a chance" — the part, it seems,
that's you, Ma — "chance" and "girl" and "give"
returning me to where all speech
began. In this place, should it jolt
feeling, a thought can be re-made.
Here strangers' cries, no longer sieved
out, disconcert a holiday.

It's not that windfall sex is out,
the sort of thing to happen to
a bishop. More that you, Ma, placed

wagers elsewhere, the tea enjoined
on visitors, the calling on
the old, the gambling ante-post
on marriage. No excursuses
having their root in privilege,
adventures up the value-chain
of feeling, blinding truths acquired,
as if by Argonauts, beyond
the limit. No — you wouldn't find
our Ma on some wild-goose chase set
insolubly by golden flesh
or fleece; nor rapt by breathing stone
in Dresden's Courtyard of the Nymphs,
if someone actual, not like
a nymph, could do with helping out.

But did your horse come in? Dark horse,
the gamble of the meeting, called
stentorianly on BBC
by Peter Bromley, moving through
the field as that kaleidoscope
in silk, those hammering hooves drowned out
by cheers, turn in at Cheltenham,
the March sun in the purple on
Cleeve Hill? In Dresden on that night
one brother died, another laboured
before the lighting of the ovens,
and prayed to understand why all
the doors of this world as they closed
did not envelop everything.
Bookies collected big, to have lived
in hope the ultimate mug's game.

This afternoon, between a plaque
explaining the "Augustus-bridge"
and ancient girders, spiders so
became themselves in weaving webs
that to compare their bridges with
our plans, their unrepined of work
with ours, was to bring on all fears.

We all do terrible things, I hear
you say, your eyes half-disengaged
and lifted to a place off-map,
*Forgiveness is a matter of
the will.* But is love instinct, more
pretension than philosophy?
I hear you say, *Pretentious, moi?*
— the hunger-striker's daughter, fan
of John Cleese and of Wodehouse, if
not an inveterate gambler on
realities unseen, then far
from being a veterate one. You must,
I know, have done with argument,
be near to someone shorn of joy
as if the very vacuum drew your love
on. Yesterday, or was it aeons
ago, your Pals' Battalion, Jenny,
Kathleen and Vivienne, sprang to
— dolloping mayonnaise on lettuce,
sprinkling their scallions pre-refined,
not going easy on the tuna,
for sandwiches so ordinary
that Death himself took shame? And we,
weak witnesses of how the casque

was heaved below to be asperged
with dust of our own hands, returned
ghosted, to find a flat alive
in sunlight, mustard on the ham,
new wine, our friends foregathering
and seeming to embody in
quotidian words their living souls?

I pay up, leave the Elbterrasse,
stroll towards the monuments of town
imagining the forest in
an age of pilgrims, innocent
of dream-encasing promenades.
I find myself within a crook
of river somewhere in the hills
of Saxony, the city not
the one that Canaletto came
to paint — no, these the terraces
and markets, parks and alley-ways
of your imagined place. Here, paths
have special signs to show the way
to foreigners. There, muted edges
protect the children — just as now,
a couple, parents, pass me by
and park their spindly pram beside
the Opera. She bends, adjusts
the bonnet on her sleeping child's
face, fingers deft as when the poet
plucked harmonies on string and shell,
and stones, trees, tigers followed him.

Two lovers in Teaterplatz,

are taking turns, footloose, hand-held,
waltzing to hidden orchestras
beyond the clouds, as much immune
to nay-saying as the half-moon
that brightens over the cathedral.
The slow Elbe swaying with heavy hips
askance of the Dimítroff bridge
is overlooked by the dark stone
of Semper's Opera: soft lights
for them too, now that they've become
an item — distant stars that pulse
unendingly. I jettison
what would dispel, dilapidate,
a moment of no consequence.
Above the river I sit down.
The lower lights are out, your life
a narrative obscure forever
— in fragments, Ma, like some old text —
and we in our perplexity
hold on to you as if to grasp
a Christmas cracker's crumpled end.
Somewhere, beyond all casting up,
that love of yours and Dad's from which
the right words come, encinctures me.
A wild rose in the ruined church;
the concave silence that degrades
our suffering and over which
our hours are strung lyre-like; the child
comforted in the dark — for us,
Ma, are the Connemara rain,
our element; a time like this
the right time for a taking leave.

INDIA

Mobilisation
(written at Sawai Madhopur Junction, Christmas Eve, 2001, as Indian forces deploy towards the border with Pakistan)

The day is half-possessed by evening.
There come strange stars

and through the junction chortling
the endless cars.

The *jawans* air their shirts, are seen
shaving or reading. Guns,

the newest missiles, tanks — all preen
in our December sun.

Before the winter can be christened spring
the mustard's fanfare

promises new things. An outspread wing
to clasp the turbid air

of sentience, the cloak that wontedly
a *sadhu* spreads, adjusts.

A legless man in hope of a rupee
shuffles our local dust.

This My Heart's Wilderness
(a response to the Persian poets who tell us that all the gold and all the women in the world are less than one man's desire)

As often as my wells are filled
by fortune, and around
me, every good is found
beloved of man on earth
— coined in gold or bound
in flesh and powerfully willed

in pleasure — nothing holds
in this my heart's wilderness,
and all my more means less:
except, in midst of dearth,
my Song, my Flower, this Yes
against harsh No, surely unfolds.

The Last Maharajah of Cochin Addresses his Jewish Subjects

These open shutters make superfluous
an old miscellany of chandeliers
and lamps. Our stockinged feet, that slip or fuss
across the Chinese tiles, are like the years

that have run on, the colloquy of rooks
along the outside wall inconsequent
as notices in Malayálam. Books,
plaques, paintings in a gallery present

iconic tales. The Romans ruled: no stone
was left upon a stone. On copperplate,
a compact with a lonely remnant blown
from Palestine before the winds. Innate

respect twelve hundred years on: *pharangis'*
rampaging fantasies, and some old Prince
rebuilds the synagogue. A life at ease,
walled and protected. Now the audience

of 1949. Those cattle trucks
like overflowing chalices are not
here. One fat Maharajah in the flux
of things almost irrelevant, a lot

of Jews with beards, reflections on a theme
of steadfastness. How soon these pioneers,
all but a few, quench lamps; and we, downstream
the cataract of Time, contribute tears!

Kalapani

My chair a pine tree's roots
as I observe
pea-hen and spotted deer
at ease among the ruins.

Something has come and gone.
On the Chief Commissioner's verandah,
tiles of Italian marble, red, black, white,
are stubbed and muddied.
On flat ground
palm trees put heads together
announcing, *No one for tennis.*
The banyan, a slew of snakes,
constricts the walls of the Subordinates Club,
will crumble them.
In the "P Church" — P for Protestant —
the roof's an open jaw
from which butterfly-like
the spirit has departed.

The colony wrote home:
A bathing picnic yesterday
at Corbyn's Cove.
The ocean is like quartz.
The new teacher, Miss Barry,
so very attractive
— as we had noticed already
at the Chief Commissioner's ball.
Six men pull our rickshaw,

each dressed in red.
They also collect tennis balls.

Shoulder-and-elbow to shoulder-and-elbow
under a forbearing sky
they sang their hymns,
their village among trees
denominated *"Paris of the East"*,
the ever-glinting ocean
their trunk road
to the Core of Things
— the whole place lifted up
by men fettered at the neck:
Bhim Rao,
Maratha peasant aged 50 years,
transported for life.
Sheik Ali,
sentenced for refusing to give information,
transported for life.
Narain, Andamans convict number 61,
excited sedition in the cantonment of Dinapore,
transported for life.
Fazal Haq,
drew up constitution for liberated Delhi,
transported for life.
Abaji Damodar,
entered into anti-British correspondence,
transported for life.
Ghulam Ghouse,
placed a wall placard in Madras
"of a highly treasonable character,"

transported for life.

These men I see before me,
a slow procession
trailing their rags and *chappals*
into the night.
They have no name,
or else a name survives
but the prisoner has undergone
confiscation of biography,
as of property.
They have no voice,
except the flogged man
screaming on the neighbour's compound.
No vindication,
for only they are to blame
— to blame for quick anger
and its exemplary punishment,
as the death-rate in Kala Pani reaches
one hundred per thousand per year,
as the authorities write home
seeking wider discretion
in the use of flogging,
as prisoners receive each day
two cups of dirty water.
The losers shake like rabbits
in the stone cells
of the Cellular Jail,
for listening to mothers or brothers
in the time that was,
and not waiting to see.

I study chipmunks
agog around an empty barrel
at the jetty
and am about to say
that all are for dumping in the end,
victor — vanquished, man — chipmunk,
when other ghosts mingle.
From Kilmainham
a delegation of shot men,
McDonagh, Plunkett, Pearse.
McDonagh, fearing "his little phrase"
will go misunderstood,
drowned out by loudness.
Pearse, knowing himself hurt to have loved
"his darling of the brave free tresses".
And then, from Reading Gaol,
comes lumbering Oscar Wilde,
the rose on his lapel
a coal on fire
amid its own life's ruin.
"If this," he states,
"is how Her Majesty
would treat her prisoners,
she doesn't deserve to have them."
His Ballad had been written off,
the Cellular Jail was coming up,
its blocks as tightly composed
as a rutting editorial
in the *Morning Post*,
when Oscar,
his dying long since underway,
descended one last time

the step-well of the soul
to bring forth
two letters about prisons.

The sand a sill of gold,
the sea caparisoned,
a thousand waves inlaid like mother-of-pearl,
the Bay a mansion, the *diwan-i-am*
in which a fleeting sun
prolongs its audience,
I rise, exclaim,
disturbing pea-hen and spotted deer
among the ruins:
One comes in glory
to judge the living and the dead.

Nobody Likes to be Born
(from the Bulgarian of Edvin Sugarev)

maybe we are
still inside the womb
maybe we are
still embryos
maybe only he is born
who is leaving,
but beyond recall

maybe we are born
of ourselves
sloughing off the placenta of the body

the Beyond, I hear
is acting as midwife

but nobody likes it,
being born.

Bewley's of Grafton Street

Not far from Bewley's,
a close-up of my father's hands
firm on the wheel of a Toyota.
He deposits me,
my future in the stars.
The light neither glares nor hides,
as when friends' mothers brought me here
after the cartoons. Paralysed,
I listen to Pascale from Strasbourg
discoursing on love.

Cinematic verity:
I meet my future wife
by prearrangement,
this doubtfully Suitable Boy
with a penchant for fried bread
and morning newspapers,
a customer to pique
the conversationally oriented
dietician
lurking in every woman.
Something starts,
or doesn't start,
as ordinary as the rain.

Before an interview,
I analyse the Celtic Tiger
— its genesis, its whereabouts, its growl —
over an unfeline diet of meringues,

and my friend and I
— a hand-held camera
with a hidden microphone
captures the whole thing —
emerge in sunlight
to find Andeans,
hair ropey and black
as Kathleen Ní Houlihan's,
a jazz band at a wedding
for all they show compunction,
their instruments a hybrid
of mountaineering gear
and primitive offensive weapons;
while painted silver,
a man from Barcelona
pretends for money
he's Charlie Chaplin's ghost.

To fast forward:
it may fall to me in the seventh age
to leave to others
the children's, lovers', public servant's tasks
and face the pages of my *Irish Times*
not needing to know.
Scenting coffee freshly drawn
from spigots
will make me mindful then
of new blood, strangers
cluttering the alcoves.
I shall imagine
my going beyond's a blip,
a train's absence

that noisily in its tunnel
premeditates the sunlight.

The final sequence of this poem
I propose to shoot by satellite
in a historic first-ever collaboration
with Latterday Roman Productions.

There you see me walking from the Green,
looking over the daffodils
on sale in Chatham Street.
You cannot tell how tired I am
as I continue in the general direction
of College Green.
You zoom in: perfect resolution,
as if some finger on the laser-guided stuff
had marked me down with a small cross.
I duck sideways,
presumably into the notorious café.
What happens next you lose.
Somewhere the collateral sound of cups and trays.
Me in voice-over, repeating:
A mere transition,
like all the smiles
on all the faces
ever God made.

Madurai Mission

Beyond a river somewhere to the west
of Madurai, at Kilaneri near
Sambukedi, her hair, his white soutane
gleam black and white. A baby, dust and tears,
grapples her neck. "Yes. There's a Christian church."

This composite of mud and smoke they call
the village. Goats crop margins, the human shoal
inert behind door-hangings. Wads of plenty
not to be wrung here from the paddy fields
or purchased out of elevated skies.

A woman bearing keys will open up
a bricks-and-mortar box. The table, cross,
and wick still smouldering in its lamp confirm
our mission. "Now, we're two small families,"
explains the key-holder. "But long before

I came here as a bride, we Christians were
quite many." Our young cicerone pronounces
"Christmas" and shunts her baby, then exclaims
"Lady of Lourdes" and laughs. "Sometimes the lot
of us, the village as a whole, come here

to pray." "The Portuguese," confides the priest,
"were like the French. They never loved our customs,
the ministry to people as they were,
in villages. That early work was lost,
and Jesuit no longer could converse

with Brahmin. Xavier had careered along
the coast, converting. Nobili became
a Tamil, waited on our thoughts, shunned all
commotion." "Uncle," interrupts our Sibyl,
"in tenth grade at the Christian school, my people

decided I should marry. And they chose
my cousin." Here, all shy, she indicates
her little boy. "You see. I'm married now."
And gaping at the startling proposition
of marigold in bloom, I apprehend

the sparrow-children of Sambukedi
surrounding us with chairs and offerings.
We extra-mural sheep are shepherded
by Robert Nobili, old ghost at hand,
purblind on grammar, catechism, love.

They serve us glasses of a milky tea.
As long ago in Rome, when letters came,
his sister in imagination reached
for that loved face, I give him less all words
to these inhabitants of wizened yards.

NOTES

Sankta Sunniva

The island of Selje north of Bergen was chosen in around 1000 A.D. as the site of the first bishopric in western Norway. The first Christian king of Norway, Olav Tryggvason, believed he had discovered there, in a cave high on the mountainside, the bodies of a group of Christians who with their leader Sunniva had perished in an avalanche when hiding from persecution a generation earlier. The tradition is firm that Sunniva and her followers came from Ireland.

A Visit To Loker Hospice Cemetery, 1990

Major William Redmond, the Nationalist MP, was killed in the advance in the Messines-Wytschaete area near Ypres on June 7th, 1917. This attack was a prelude to "third Ypres", the battle of summer and autumn 1917 in which casualties on the British side alone numbered 300,000. Redmond was brought in wounded from no-man's land by stretcher-bearers of the Ulster Division and died several hours later. Shortly after the end of the First World War, Redmond's remains were transferred at the request of his relatives to a separate plot some yards from the war cemetery at Loker Hospice. This was to emphasise, against a background of political turmoil in Ireland, that Redmond served in the war as an Irish patriot and that his goals of building bridges to the Unionists and securing Home Rule remained unfulfilled. To this day Redmond's grave is outside the official cemetery.

Kalapani

The first prison colony in the Andamans was set up at the end of the 18th century. The colony was re-established to cater for the large numbers entering the prison system in the years following the rebellion of 1857. Early in the 20th century, a system based on island camps was replaced by the Cellular Jail, a fortress-style prison in the main settlement at Port Blair. From mid-nineteenth century until the years preceding Indian independence, a sentence of transportation for life to these prisons across the Bay of Bengal was known as "Kala Pani" or "black water"; it is said that the name arose because to cross the ocean or "black water" was at any time unpropitious. In the same period, Ross Island, just opposite Port Blair, was the elegant headquarters of the colonial administration.

Madurai Mission

Robert Nobili (or di Nobili) was born in Rome in 1577, the illegitimate son of a wealthy nobleman. In 1596 he entered the Jesuits - for which purpose he will have been obliged to conceal his illegitimate birth. Having hesitated between India and Japan, Nobili opted for the India mission and arrived in Portuguese Goa in 1605. Nobili was in Goa for several months, at the "professed house", among the parishes of South Goa, and in the infirmary of the Jesuit school (his health was to remain precarious; he was said not to have been well for a single day of his long career in India). In Goa it is practically certain that Nobili met Thomas Stephens, an English Jesuit who had been the companion of Edmund Campion who died at Tyburn. Stephens was already the pioneer, in India, of an approach to missionary work based on the attempt to master thoroughly the local language and culture - which in turn implied peaceful relations with the Brahmins.

On transfer to the mission at Madurai, Nobili began his lifelong engagement with south Indian language and culture, especially Tamil. His adoption of the extremely ascetic life of an Indian holy man caused a falling out with his fellow Jesuits and contributed further to his ill-health. Nobili was soon obliged by his colleagues to set up a separate mission at Madurai outside the Jesuit mainstream. Defending the wearing of the thread, a Hindu observance, by himself and other Christians, Nobili wrote that the earliest Christians had been allowed to frequent the Jewish temple. Nobili's knowledge of Tamil enabled him to demonstrate that Christian theology, as taught by his predecessors in South India, had been garbled in transmission. Drawing on the theories of Roman rhetoric, he challenged his fellow missionaries to answer the question, "By what right do we expect the Hindus to listen to us?" A saying of Nobili's (from the Book of Kings) was "deus non est in commotione": God is not found in uproar.

Nobili had the support of his own bishop, an imaginative Spaniard. However, the "Madurai method" became extremely controversial among the Jesuits and the bishops generally. In 1619 Nobili was summoned to Goa to account for himself before a special convention of the Catholic church in India. Despite the tremendous defence mounted by his bishop and by himself (of which documentation survives), Robert Nobili was heavily outvoted and forbidden to continue his work.

At this point Ireland enters the story. Nobili appealed to the Pope over the head of the Catholic church in India. The Pope appointed a commission under the Archbishop of Armagh, Peter Lombard, to make a definitive ruling on the "Madurai method". Lombard's sympathies were clear. Using his casting vote, he enabled Robert Nobili's Madurai mission to continue. This was in 1623. Nobili was to continue working, at Madurai, Jaffna, and Mylapore, until his death in 1657. For the last several years of his life he was completely blind.

On Robert Nobili's death the "Madurai method" ran into the sands - as happened also to the analogous approach of Matteo Ricci in China. Nobili mastered six languages (Latin, Italian, Portuguese, Tamil, Telegu, Kannada) and is remembered today as a figure in the history of Tamil literature. His role as a Christian theologian and evangelist is perhaps not as widely recognised. Nobili's originality has always been under suspicion from conservatives. At the same time some of those who sympathise in principle with a bolder theology ask whether his conciliatory attitude to Hindus and Hindu rulers involved too much compromise with the caste system.

Nobili is best known to western audiences through Vincent Cronin's novel, "A Pearl For India" (1959). A more accurate account of his life is "A Star In The East" by Fr. S. Rajamanickam S.J., (Madras 1995). My Foreign Affairs colleague Gearóid O Broin makes a fresh contribution to our understanding of Nobili in his article "The Family Background Of Robert Nobili" (Archivum Historicum Societatis Jesu, 1999). Ambassador O Broin demonstrates that Nobili was illegitimate, a thesis hitherto resisted by Jesuit scholars. O Broin also brings to light the violence, corruption, and intrigue that marked the milieu of the Nobili family in 16th century Rome.